ASWAN

EGYPT POCKET GUIDE

Alberto Siliotti

THE AMERICAN UNIVERSITY IN CAIRO PRESS

Text and Photographs Alberto Siliotti
Drawings Stefania Cossu
English Translation CTM (Italy)

General Editing Yvonne Marzoni
Graphic Design Geodia

Copyright © 2002 by Geodia (Verona, Italy)

This edition first published in Egypt jointly by
The American University in Cairo Press (Cairo and New York)
Elias Modern Publishing House (Cairo)
Geodia (Verona, Italy)

Created by Geodia (Verona, Italy)
Printed in Egypt by Elias Modern Publishing House (Cairo)
Distributed by the American University in Cairo Press (Cairo and New York)

ISBN 977 424 642 X   Dar el Kutub No. 17883/00

In the text "(⇨ X)" means "go to page X"

Contents

Trajan's kiosk on the island of Philae

Spices in the Aswan souk

The temple of Horus at Edfu

The hill of Qubbet al-Hawa and the Tombs of the Nobles at Aswan

From Luxor to Aswan

The temple of Montu at Tod

*T*his trip can be made either on land or by boat up the Nile and allows for visits to all the major archeological sites.

After leaving Luxor and crossing the new bridge (named 'Nile Bridge') that makes a visit to the necropolises and temples of Western Thebes much simpler, the first archeological site on the journey to Aswan is **Tod**. This is the location of a small temple dedicated to Montu that was built during the reign of Sesostris (1964–1919 BC) but renovated during the Ptolemaic period. In 1936, an important treasure was discovered here that is now exhibited in the Egyptian Museum in Cairo and the Louvre in Paris. A few kilometers

The famous golden falcon head, the emblem of the god Horus, discovered at Hierakonpolis (Egyptian Museum, Cairo)

The mysterious pyramid of al-Kula

farther on, **Gebelein** ("the two hills") on the west bank is the site of a large city with necropolises from the Old Kingdom and First Intermediate Period in which very important finds were made that are now displayed in Turin Museum. Next comes **Esna**, still on the west bank, where the lovely temple of Khnum (⇨ **6**) stands completely surrounded by the modern village.
Farther south, and on the east bank, one reaches the site of **al-Kab** which was the ancient city of *Nekheb*, where there is an important necropolis from the Middle Kingdom

(⇨ **8**). On the other side of the river from al-Kab stands the small pyramid of **al-Kula** which was probably built during the Third Dynasty, and, close to the village of **Kom al-Ahmar** ("the red hill"), the remains of Nekhen, which the Greeks called

The ancient enclosure walls of pharaoh Khasekhemuwy at Kom al-Ahmar

Hierakonpolis ("the city of the falcon"), as it was the seat of the cult of the falcon Horus. Nekhen was the capital of Egypt during the pre-Dynastic period and it was here that the famous Tablet of Narmer, now in the Egyptian Museum in Cairo, was discovered. The ruins of a massive enclosure wall, probably built for funerary use during the reign of Khasekhemwy, the last ruler of the Second

The rock temple of Horemheb at Gebel Silsila

Dynasty (first half of the third millennium BC) are still visible. From here one continues to the town of **Edfu**, halfway between Luxor and Aswan, where the Ptolemaic temple of

The large sandstone caves at Gebel Silsila

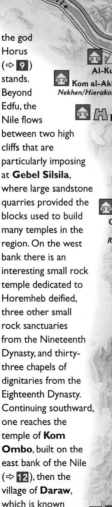

the god Horus (⇨ 9) stands. Beyond Edfu, the Nile flows between two high cliffs that are particularly imposing at **Gebel Silsila**, where large sandstone quarries provided the blocks used to build many temples in the region. On the west bank there is an interesting small rock temple dedicated to Horemheb deified, three other small rock sanctuaries from the Nineteenth Dynasty, and thirty-three chapels of dignitaries from the Eighteenth Dynasty. Continuing southward, one reaches the temple of **Kom Ombo**, built on the east bank of the Nile (⇨ 12), then the village of **Daraw**, which is known

The camel market in Daraw

for its picturesque market where camels from Sudan are bought and sold; the market is especially busy on Tuesdays and Sundays. Forty kilometers or so more will bring you to Aswan (⇨ 16).

LUXOR — Km 0
Al-Bayadiya
Armant
— Km 8
Nile Bridge (Bridge of Luxor)
Tod — Km 21
Gebelein — Km 28
Al-Moalla *Hefat*
Dam of Esna Bridge of Esna — Km 54
ESNA *Latopolis* *Temple of Khnum*
Al-Sibaiya
Nile
Al-Kab — Km 86 *Nekheb/Eileithyaspolis*
Al-Kula
Kom al-Akhmar *Nekhen/Hierakonpolis*
Marsa Alam
EDFU — Km 105 Bridge of Edfu
Gebel Silsila (West) *Rock temple of Horemheb*
Gebel Silsila (East) — Km 146
KOM OMBO — Km 163 *Temple of Sobek & Haroeri*
Daraw — Km 171
2, 7
Camel market
ASWAN — Km 209
Is. of Elephantine
PHILAE

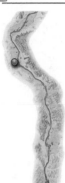

Esna

*T*he temple at Esna was dedicated to Khnum, an ancient god of creation who shaped humanity on his potter's wheel using clay from the Nile; it was one of the last of the great Egyptian temples to be built.

The facade of the temple in Esna built during the Roman period

The temple at Esna was mainly dedicated to Khnum whose cult was associated with that of Neith, a warlike goddess, who in turn was worshipped with the lioness-goddess Menhyt and the goddess Heka. The building stands in the center of the modern town in a huge four-sided depression, 9 meters lower than the level of the current city streets; the city Ta-Senet (from which the modern name Esna is derived) was the capital of the third nome of Upper Egypt and known to the Greeks as *Latopolis* ("the city of Lates" in reference to the Nile perch *Lates niloticus* considered sacred). The perfectly preserved part of the building that is visible today is the hypostyle hall that dates from the time of the Roman emperor Claudius (41–54 AD) who enlarged an earlier structure built during the reign of Ptolemy VI (180–145 BC). It was originally connected to a landing stage on the Nile (still visible) by a

Emperor Titus is purified by the gods Harsiesi and Thoth

The elegant capitals of the columns in the hypostyle hall in the temple

processional way. The oldest architectural element in the temple is the west wall of the hypostyle hall, whose Roman ceiling is still intact. The rectangular room has twenty-four columns crowned by extremely

Low relief depicting the creation of man

The temple of Esna as it was during the Roman period

finely-worked capitals in sixteen different forms. The shafts of the columns are decorated with low reliefs and texts referring to the three principal festivals in

Plan of the temple of Esna

the liturgical calendar of the temple; these correspond to the creation of the world by the goddess Neith, the raising of the sky by Khnum, and the god's victory over rebellious man. Two interesting cryptographic texts transcribe two hymns to the god Khnum using mainly hieroglyphs of rams and crocodiles. The decoration of the hypostyle hall was continually enriched until the reign of the Roman emperor Decius in the third century AD. The ceiling is decorated with astronomical motifs that represent the course of the sun and the constellations in the heavenly vault.

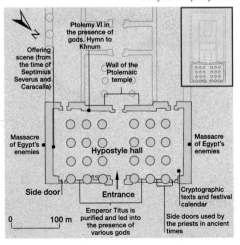

Ptolemy VI in the presence of gods. Hymn to Khnum

Offering scene (from the time of Septimius Severus and Caracalla)

Wall of the Ptolemaic temple

Massacre of Egypt's enemies

Hypostyle hall

Massacre of Egypt's enemies

Side door

Entrance

Cryptographic texts and festival calendar

0   100 m

Emperor Titus is purified and led into the presence of various gods

Side doors used by the priests in ancient times

Al-Kab

Practically ignored by tourists, al-Kab is an archeological site of prime importance and the tombs in its Middle Kingdom necropolis are decorated with superb low reliefs.

A low relief in Paheri's tomb showing the harvest and the preparation of wine

Situated on the right bank of the Nile opposite *Nekhen*, the ancient city of *Nekheb* (*Eileithyaspolis* to the Greeks) was the center of the cult of the vulture goddess Nekhbet, the guardian deity of Upper Egypt. The solid walls of the city are still visible and contain the remains of two small temples from the Eighteenth Dynasty and those of the large temple dedicated to Nekhbet; the latter was also from the Eighteenth Dynasty but was rebuilt during the Twenty-fifth and Thirtieth Dynasties. There are, however, many indications of much more ancient inhabitance: human beings have lived here since the seventh millennium BC. On

the cliff to the east of the town there are many rock tombs decorated with beautiful polychrome low reliefs that are the most interesting archeological aspect of the area. The tombs most worthy of note are those of Paheri

(no. 3), the "mayor of the city" during the reign of Ahmose (1550–1525 BC), the founder of the Eighteenth Dynasty, and that of Ahmose, the son of Ebana (no. 2), who is famous for his accounts of the defeat of the Hyksos invaders. A small Ptolemaic rock temple and a chapel of Amenophis III are situated southward.

The chapel of Amenophis III

Plan of al-Kab

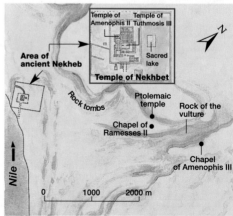

The Temple of Horus at Edfu

The temple of the falcon god Horus at Edfu is the best preserved of all Egyptian temples; its walls are completely covered with hieroglyphic texts, thus forming an extraordinary library.

The falcon god Horus

The first pylon in the Ptolemaic temple of Horus at Edfu (36 meters high by 80 meters wide)

Edfu was the ancient city *Djeba*, known to the Greeks as *Apollinopolis Magna*. It was the capital of the second nome in Upper Egypt and a great commercial center at the end of a long trade route that connected the Nile with the Red Sea. Egyptian legend told that this was the site of the battle between the falcon-god Horus and the evil god Seth, who was responsible for the death of Horus' father, Osiris.

The great temple dedicated to Horus stands in the center of the modern town. Construction began in 237 BC during the reign of Ptolemy III (246–221 BC) on the remains of an earlier structure from the New Kingdom. The work

The granite statue of Horus wearing the double crown of Upper and Lower Egypt in front of the hypostyle hall

lasted for 180 years overall, having continued at various times during the reigns of Ptolemy IV (221–204 BC), Ptolemy VIII (145–116 BC), who completed the hypostyle atrium, and Ptolemy XII (80–51 BC) who finished the decoration of the building in 57 BC. The exceptional state of preservation of the construction—the largest Ptolemaic temple of all—gives visitors the impression that the priests have only just abandoned the site. In fact, the temple remained almost completely buried by the sand until 1860 when excavation was begun by

The pharaoh offers an image of Maat, the goddess of cosmic order (indicated by the arrow), to Horus and Hathor

the French archeologist Auguste Mariette, the director of the Egyptian Museum in Cairo. Forty years were needed for the Egyptologists Maxence de Rochemonteix and Émile Chassinat to write

construction. The temple comprises an impressive pylon (in front of which there stands a small birth house or *mammisi*, a temple in which celebrations took place of the birth of Harsomtus, the son of Horus and Hathor) decorated with dual scenes of the ritual massacre of enemies by Ptolemy XII before Horus. The pylon is followed by a four-sided court bordered on the south, east, and west sides by a 32–column portico and on the north side by a hypostyle atrium

or *pronaos* (also commonly referred to as the first hypostyle hall). The famous statue of Horus in the form of a falcon stands in front of the pronaos. The low reliefs in the court show the most important festival in the temple, the "festival of the good meeting" during which the statue of the goddess Hathor in Dendera was transported by river to visit Horus in Edfu. The hypostyle atrium is decorated on the outer wall with scenes of offerings by the pharaoh to

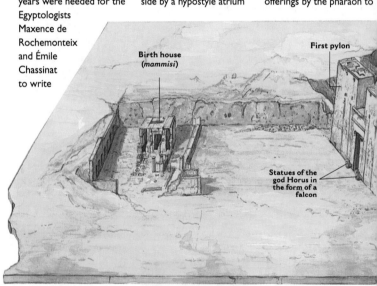

Birth house (*mammisi*)

First pylon

Statues of the god Horus in the form of a falcon

and publish, between 1897 and 1934, a colossal work of fourteen volumes that contained an epigraphic survey of all the hieroglyphic texts in the temple, thus forming a real library in stone.
The current building has a north–south orientation, not east–west as is usually the case in temple

The mammisi *or "temple of divine birth" whose construction was probably begun during the reign of Ptolemy VIII*

Model of Horus' sacred bark in one of the chapels

scenes that commemorate the founding of the temple in 237 BC, and with images of the sacred barks of Horus and Hathor. Entering deeper into the temple, the height of the ceilings and the amount of light that enters are progressively reduced. One passes through the room in which food offerings were placed, the vestibule in which the barks of the gods in the river processions were deposited and, lastly, into the sanctuary, at the back of which stands the granitoid monolithic shrine from the age of Nectanebo II (359–341 BC) where the statue of Horus was placed.

Horus and Hathor, and its ceiling is supported by twelve large columns on which all the most important divinities of Egypt are portrayed. In a small recess (known as a

Hieroglyphic texts on the walls of the library state the titles of the papyruses that were originally available, of which, unfortunately, not one remains. On the other side

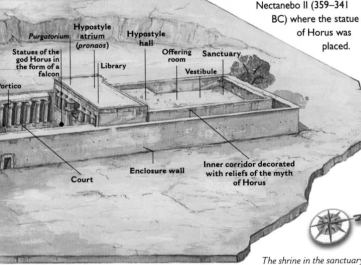
Three-dimensional representation of the temple of Horus in Edfu

Labels on the diagram: Purgatorium; Hypostyle atrium (pronaos); Hypostyle hall; Statues of the god Horus in the form of a falcon; Offering room; Sanctuary; Library; Vestibule; Portico; Court; Enclosure wall; Inner corridor decorated with reliefs of the myth of Horus

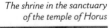

The shrine in the sanctuary of the temple of Horus

purgatorium) to the left of the entrance, the priest performed rites of purification, and in a similar space to the left (referred to as the "library"), the temple papyruses were stored and the purified priest read the texts relating to the liturgy of the day.

of the hypostyle atrium, one enters the hypostyle hall, which also has twelve columns with differently-formed capitals. The walls are decorated with images of the gods worshipped in the temple (to whom are dedicated the eleven chapels that surround the central sanctuary), with

Kom Ombo

Situated on a hill on the east bank of the Nile, the fascinating temple of Kom Ombo was dedicated to two gods: the crocodile god Sobek and the falcon god Haroeris.

The crocodile god Sobek

The hypostyle hall in the Ptolemaic temple at Kom Ombo

temple has a particular appeal. The name Kom Ombo means "the hill of Ombos" and was the ancient city of *Pa-Sobek* ("the possession of Sobek"). Its temple was probably built over the remains of other buildings from the Middle and New Kingdoms and is the only known example of a temple divided into two parts along its longitudinal axis. These were dedicated to the crocodile

Although it was plundered for its building materials during the Coptic era, half-buried by sand, and its western section partially eroded by the flooding of the Nile, the Ptolemaic

above and some dozens of meters from the Nile, on a wide bend before the island of Mansuria, the

temple of Kom Ombo still stands halfway between Edfu and Aswan, about four kilometers from the village of Kom Ombo. Built on the east bank

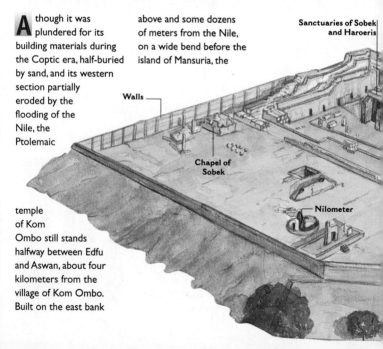

Sanctuaries of Sobek and Haroeris

Walls

Chapel of Sobek

Nilometer

god Sobek and the falcon god Haroeris, who was a form of Horus known as "Horus the Ancient." Sobek was associated with his consort Hathor and their son Khonsu, while Haroeris was associated with Tasenetnofret ("The Good Sister") and their son Panebtaui "(Lord of the Two Lands"). Construction of the temple began during the reign of Ptolemy VI (180–145 BC), when Ombos had become a town of some importance, and was completed by Ptolemy XII (80–51 BC); the court and the enclosure wall were decorated during the Roman period. A *mammisi*, which is

The falcon god Haroeris

annexed to the temple, was built during the reign of Ptolemy IX (116–107 BC) in the northwest corner of the court, right by the Nile. The complex plan of the temple is aligned on the traditional east–west axis and reflects the fact it was built to worship two gods. At one time it had a pylon with a double entrance, but only its remains can be seen now. Other elements of the complex include a hypostyle atrium, a transverse hypostyle hall, three transverse vestibules and two sanctuaries. All these structures are surrounded by a double enclosure wall and two corridors: the inner one opens into the first

hypostyle atrium, the outer into the court. Similar to the temple at Edfu, the outer corridor is decorated with low reliefs. There is a famous relief in the eastern

Low reliefs depicting surgical instruments

section that shows a series of objects traditionally interpreted as surgical instruments, though some scholars consider them to be instruments related to ritual practices, due to the

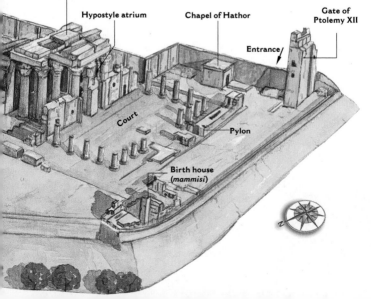

Three-dimensional representation of the temple of Kom Ombo

Vestibules
Hypostyle hall
Hypostyle atrium
Chapel of Hathor
Gate of Ptolemy XII
Entrance
Court
Pylon
Birth house (*mammisi*)

fact that many faithful made the pilgrimage to this temple to ask Haroeris to cure them of their infirmity. The current entrance to the temple is through a passage in the ruins of the great entrance portal originally built by Ptolemy XII. Only the eastern section and a chapel dedicated to Hathor by the Roman emperor Domitian (51–96 AD) remain. The temple contains several mummified crocodiles that were found in a nearby necropolis.

The small chapel of Hathor, from the Roman period, on the south side of the temple

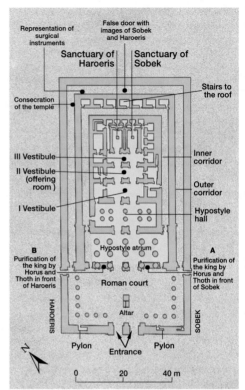

Plan of the temple of Kom Ombo

After passing through the entrance, one enters the court constructed during the reign of Tiberius (14–27 AD). It is surrounded on three sides by sixteen columns, of which only parts of shafts remain, which are decorated with polychrome low reliefs. The court is divided into

Hieroglyph representing the god Sobek

two sections: in the center there is a small double altar where offerings were made to the two gods. The east side of the court is formed by the facade of the hypostyle atrium (pronaos) which is adorned on its upper section by the traditional Egyptian molding of winged sun disks flanked by uraeus serpents, and below, a dedicatory inscription by Ptolemy XII. Three large columns with composite capitals mark the boundary of the dual-entrance gateway that gives access to the hypostyle atrium.

One of the reliefs on the columns of the court showing the goddess Nekhbet protecting the cartouches of the emperor Tiberius

The low reliefs on either side of the doors show the purification of Ptolemy XII by Horus and Thoth in the presence of Sobek on the right (**A**) and Haroeris on the left (**B**). The atrium is also divided in two parts by three columns with composite capitals. The remaining columns are in the form of papyrus plants with open capitals and have shafts decorated with scenes of offerings. The wall reliefs in the atrium are in keeping with the theme of coronation. From here one enters the adjacent hypostyle room which has papyrus-shaped columns and is somewhat smaller than the atrium. The low reliefs in this part of the temple depict the purification and coronation of Ptolemy VIII (145–116 BC) who receives the sword of victory from Haroeris. Three transverse vestibules without columns follow: in the first, the low reliefs portray the foundation and purification of the temple while in the

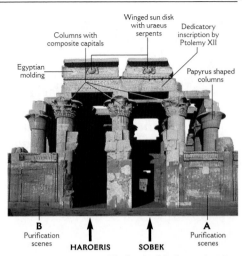

Winged sun disk with uraeus serpents
Columns with composite capitals
Dedicatory inscription by Ptolemy XII
Egyptian molding
Papyrus shaped columns
B Purification scenes
HAROERIS
SOBEK
A Purification scenes

The facade of the hypostyle atrium

second, sometimes referred to as the "offering room," they represent the daily cult activities and offerings made to the gods.

A third vestibule precedes the sanctuaries of Sobek and Haroeris, which are both in a very poor state.

Inside it is possible to see the platforms on which the sacred barks of the gods were placed. The two sanctuaries are surrounded by a number of chapels.

A false door in the outer corridor, decorated with images of Sobek and Haroeris, is on a level with the two sanctuaries. On the north side of the temple, there is a deep well with a complex structure that was used to supply the priests with pure water for their ablutions.

The well on the north side of the temple

The papyrus-shaped columns in the first hypostyle hall

Aswan

Aswan, the ancient city of Syene, was the largest trading center in the Nile Valley. It was the point at which goods from equatorial Africa and the Mediterranean were exchanged.

Elephantine Island, which faces modern Aswan; it used to be the ancient trading center of the city at the level of the First Cataract on the river Nile

The Greeks called Aswan *Syene*, which they took from the Egyptian word *swenet* meaning "trade." The city was the largest trading center for products from equatorial Africa and the Nile Valley.

The ancient city did not originally lie on the right bank of the Nile, where the modern city is, but on Elephantine (⇨ **20**), the island opposite the town, in the First Cataract of the Nile, which was a natural barrier that proved an insurmountable obstacle

Feluccas are characteristic Egyptian sailing boats and the symbol of Aswan

to river traffic (⇨ **23**). The city was built on Elephantine Island for security reasons: the island could easily be defended, which was essential as it was at the southern tip of pharaonic Egypt, beyond which the "*land of Kush*" began, i.e. Nubia.

During the Ptolemaic period, the inhabited area spread to the east bank but no trace remains of these settlements as they have since been covered by the modern city, with the exceptions of a temple dedicated to Isis

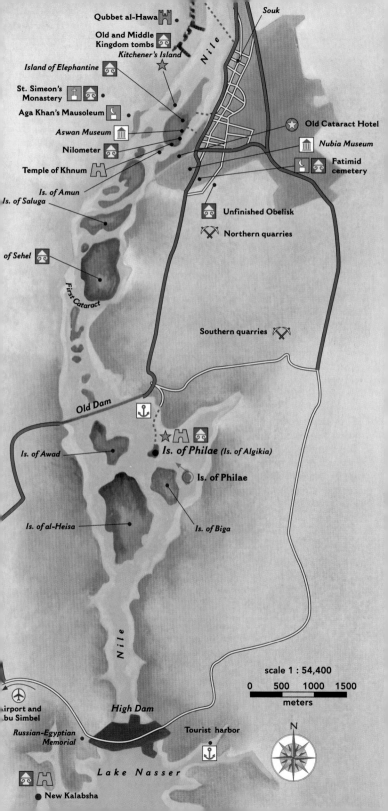

Qubbet al-Hawa

Old and Middle
Kingdom tombs

Kitchener's Island

Island of Elephantine

St. Simeon's
Monastery

Aga Khan's Mausoleum

Aswan Museum

Nilometer

Temple of Khnum

Is. of Amun

Is. of Saluga

of Sehel

First Cataract

Souk

Nile

Old Cataract Hotel

Nubia Museum

Fatimid
cemetery

Unfinished Obelisk

Northern quarries

Southern quarries

Old Dam

Is. of Awad

Is. of Philae (Is. of Algikia)

Is. of Philae

Is. of al-Heisa

Is. of Biga

Nile

scale 1 : 54,400

0   500   1000   1500

meters

Airport and
bu Simbel

*Russian-Egyptian
Memorial*

High Dam

Tourist harbor

N

Lake Nasser

New Kalabsha

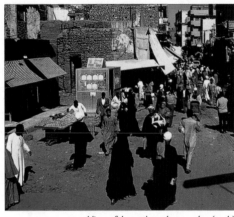

View of Aswan's modern market (souk)

built during the reigns of Ptolemy III (246–221 BC) and Ptolemy IV (221–204 BC), and a small Roman temple built by Domitian and dedicated to the gods of the cataract (Khnum, Satet, and Anuket).

The development of modern Aswan began at the end of the nineteenth century as a base for British troops after their occupation of Egypt in 1882. It was from Aswan that the

military operations began that led to the defeat of the Mahdist rebels and

Alexandria. The city enjoys a typically African climate, dry and warm in the winter (there is an average difference of about 18°F between Cairo and Aswan), and hot but breezy during the summer.

The **modern market** (the *souk*) is one of the largest and most important in Egypt and unquestionably the most picturesque; it clearly shares the same character seen in the culture of modern Nubia. A long series of small shops and peddlers

Aswan's spice market has a certain importance even today

Aswan is one of the main producers of karkadé, *a typical Egyptian drink made by infusing dried hibiscus flowers* (Hibiscus esculentus)

conquest of Sudan under Lord Horatio Herbert Kitchener in 1898.

In 1925 the population of Aswan was only 15,000 but today, with 500,000 inhabitants, it is the third largest city in Egypt after Cairo and

winds for over two kilometers along Sharia el Souk ("market street"), which runs parallel to the road along the Nile. Spices, colored fabrics of all kinds, fruit, vegetables, *karkadé*, meat, rugs, and local handmade products are the most common items, which are aimed more at the local inhabitants than the tourists. One of Egypt's most famous hotels, the **Old Cataract Hotel**, has stood at the southern end of the city since the end of the nineteenth century. Nearby is the **Nubia Museum** (⇨ **42**), built with the aid of UNESCO and opened in 1997, and an important **Islamic cemetery** from the era of the Fatimid dynasty (969–1171 AD). The many tombs, some of which belonged to the

The Old Cataract Hotel is a famous site in Aswan

architectural viewpoint, the elaborate domes and arches are typical

One of the tombs in the monumental Fatimid cemetery in Aswan

Arab governors of the city, were built with unbaked bricks. From an

elements of the tombs. Farther to the southeast are the **pink granite**

quarries (⇨ **26**) that provided many of the building materials for the main cult centers in pharaonic Egypt.

A few kilometers farther south, the Nile is interrupted by the **Old Dam** and then the **High Dam** (⇨ **24**).

The famous **island of Philae** (⇨ **34**) lies between the two of them.

On the west bank, opposite the modern city, are the large **monastery of St. Simeon** (⇨ **28**) and what are referred to as the **"tombs of the nobles"** (⇨ **30**).

General view of the west bank of the Nile

Elephantine

*E*lephantine was the largest trading center in Nubia and an important religious center that worshipped the goddess Satet, her consort Khnum, and their daughter Anuket.

Relief of the god Khnum with a ram's head

View of the temple of Satet after restoration work

The island Elephantine was initially the center of the economic, religious, and political life of Aswan because its position in the middle of the Nile, just downstream from the First Cataract, made it easy to defend and an ideal place to control river traffic. The capital of Upper Egypt's first nome, the island was called Ibu, which was a word that meant "elephant," a clear reference to the trade in ivory from the lands of Upper Nubia (in modern Sudan). It has been inhabited since the fourth millennium BC (the period of the Naqada II culture) and acquired substantial importance during the Old Kingdom at the time of the Sixth Dynasty (2321–2140 BC). This was the period in which the sanctuary of Heqaib was built. He was the most famous governor of the city, (his tomb is in the necropolis on the west bank) and was deified after his death. Elephantine was increasingly prosperous in the Middle and New Kingdoms and continued to be the site of a garrison during the Graeco-Roman period. Elephantine's **archeological area** is

Statue of an elephant in the southern part of the island

Plan of Elephantine Island

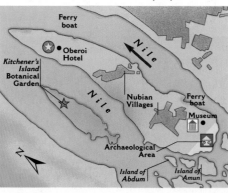

Aswan

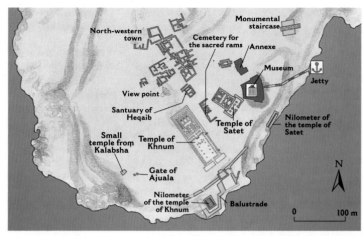

Plan of the archeological area of Elephantine Island

the location of the island's ancient settlement, which covers an area of 2 square kilometers on the southern end of the island. Excavation began in 1969 under the aegis of the German Institute of Archeology in collaboration with the Swiss Institute for Archeological Research and has uncovered the temple of Satet—the main deity of the island, with whom her consort Khnum and the goddess Anuket were later associated—whose cult center lay on the nearby island of Sehel. The temple dates to the reigns of Hatshepsut (1479–1457 BC) and Thutmose III (1479–1425 BC). In the center of the island (500 meters long) there are two **Nubian**

The historic building that houses the archeological museum

A typical Nubian village on Elephantine Island

villages, characterized by brightly colored houses, and the **archeological museum** is located in southeast section. This building, constructed in 1902, was originally the home of Sir William Wilcocks, the designer of the Old Dam.
A number of objects found during excavation are exhibited here, though the most important ones have been transferred to the new Nubia Museum (⇨ 42).

The famous Nilometer on Elephantine Island, seen from the river

The famous **Nilometer** stands close to the museum and was used to measure the varying levels of the Nile in order to predict the extent of annual flooding. This was recorded in the kingdom's annals and used to judge the success of the crops, which were the basis of the country's economy. The taxation system was also calculated on the basis of the water level and potential of the annual flood.

The current Nilometer is in a perfect state of preservation (it was still in use in 1870), having been rebuilt during the late Ptolemaic and Roman period. It was perhaps based on an earlier, similar structure annexed to the temple of Satet. Its original measuring scale can be read in Greek characters with Arabic numbers beside it and a modern metric scale is carved on pieces of marble. Farther south lie the remains of a second, more ancient Nilometer, associated with the great temple of Khnum, the main religious building on the island, which was described by the Greek geographer Strabo during his journey in Egypt in the first

enlarged during the reigns of Nectanebo I (378–360 BC), Nectanebo II (359–341 BC), and in the Graeco-Roman period. Today the only parts to be seen are the foundations. Excavations made from 1906–09 between the temples of Satet and Khnum unearthed the necropolis of the Sacred Rams in which mummified rams covered with cartonnage sheathed in gold were found. One of them is now displayed in the Nubia Museum (⇨ **46**). Finally, a small

The Nilometer on Elephantine Island with the graduated notches that indicate the level of the river

century BC.

The temple of Khnum was originally built during the New Kingdom and

temple from the reign of the Meroitic king Hergamenes II (218–196 BC), originally built at Kalabsha, was reconstructed right on the southern tip of the island in 1972, and the gateway of the temple of Ajuala (a locality near Kalabsha, today submerged by the waters of Lake Nasser) was reconstructed close by in 1988. Not far away is a granite statue of an elephant that was found in 1987 during excavation of the temple of Isis in Aswan.

The small Ptolemaic temple on the southern tip of the island, coming from the site of Kalabsha

The Cataract

Votive stele on the island of Sehel to the gods of the cataract, Khnum, Satet, and Anuket

The First Cataract, now waterless, is very different than how it was in the past

*O*nce an almost insurmountable obstacle of rushing Nile water, the First Cataract is now a peaceful scene, the perfect location for a late afternoon felucca ride.

Upstream from Elephantine (⇨ **20**) as far as the island of Al-Heisa, the Nile is interrupted for about five kilometers by blocks of granite of different size and shape that, due to a drop in height, the river used to rush against, throwing up high plumes of spray in a deafening roar.

This is how travelers in the nineteenth century described the cataract (from the Greek *katarraktés* meaning waterfall). Today the reduction in water flow, consequent upon the construction of the two dams, has meant the cataract (in Arabic *shellal*) has lost its original appearance, leaving many of the granite boulders permanently high and dry. On the island of Sehel, lying in the middle of the First Cataract,

The "Famine Stele" on the island of Sehel

more than 200 stelae and graffiti from the pharaonic period, and the famous "Famine Stele" from the Ptolemaic period, were found. Its texts, arranged vertically, narrate the terrible famine that afflicted the country during the reign of Djoser, around 2600 BC, following the failure of the floods over a period of seven years.

The cataract in a nineteenth century engraving

The High Dam

*T*he Aswan High Dam is one of the greatest works of hydraulic engineering of the twentieth century and has profoundly altered the economic development and agriculture of Egypt, but also the environment of the entire Nile Valley.

Aerial view of the High Dam in Aswan

Between 1899 and 1902, the British built what is now called the Old Dam. Its control of the waters allowed the area of cultivated land to be increased by about 10% but also caused the partial flooding of many Nubian villages and the monuments on the island of Philae, which remained almost completely covered with water for much of the year. The need to increase the production of electrical energy and the quantity of water available for agriculture prompted President Nasser to build a second, much larger, dam. Work on the High Dam (*al-Sadd al-Aali* in Arabic) began in 1960 with the financial and technical help of the Soviet Union and was inaugurated in 1971 by President Nasser.

The dam itself is indeed

Plan of the High Dam in Aswan

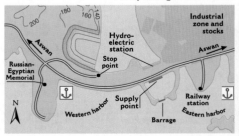

The hydroelectric station on the High Dam

disadvantages, including the loss of important pharaonic monuments and a large number of Nubian villages, whose inhabitants were forced to move elsewhere. No one, however, had fully considered the effects the High Dam would have on the environment not only of Egypt but also the Mediterranean basin over one thousand kilometers away.

pharaonic: its mass is seventeen times that of the pyramid of Khufu! And for the first time in 5,000 years, the Egyptians were able to have complete control of the waters of the Nile. The construction of the dam also meant that for the first time, the annual inundation, the flooding of the river that had always regulated the life and human activities in the Nile Valley and had made the soil fertile by washing between 60 and 180 million tons of nutritious silt down the river valley, was halted. In contrast to the unquestionable benefits deriving from the project, there were also many

The Old Dam built in 1902

THE HIGH DAM IN FIGURES

Height: 111 m
Length (at the top): 3.6 km
Width (at the base): 980 m
Volume: 55.8 million cubic yards
Time required for its construction: 11 years
Hydroelectric energy produced: 10 billion kwh

The Aswan High Dam has had an enormous impact on the environment. Today it is possible to draw up a balance of its positive and negative points.

➕	➖
1. Protection from possible flooding.	1. Disappearance of the fertilizing effect of the silt deposited on the flooded agricultural fields.
2. Creation of a large reservoir of water for agricultural development of the country.	2. Erosion of the Mediterranean coast due to the lack of silt washed down.
3. Production of hydroelectric energy that fulfills a quarter of the country's requirements.	3. An increase in the pollution of the waters of the Nile.
	4. An increase in the humidity over all Egypt, and a rise in the water table.

Russian-Egyptian monument

The Unfinished Obelisk

*T*he obelisk at Aswan would have been the largest of all Egyptian obelisks, but its construction was abandoned, probably because of the appearance of a fissure in its shaft.

The enormous unfinished obelisk, estimated to weigh about 1,200 tons

Roughly six kilometers southeast of Aswan, beyond the Fatimid cemetery, lie the granite quarries which were already famous during the Old Kingdom and were still being used during the Roman era. One of the quarries contains a gigantic obelisk that was perfectly cut out of the rock, but which was abandoned when it was nearly complete. If it had been finished, at 42.5 meters high it would have exceeded by 10 meters the already gigantic

"unique obelisk of the east" from Karnak temple, which was transported to Rome c. 330 AD and erected in the Piazza di San Giovanni in Laterano. It is calculated that the weight of the unfinished obelisk in Aswan is about 1,200 tons.

Study of the obelisk—which attracts a great number of tourists every day—has provided important information on the techniques used by ancient builders. In the rock around the obelisk it is still possible to see the

marks of the chisels and the places where wedges of palm wood were placed at regular intervals by the workers. These were then soaked so that they would expand and crack the rock.

*The obelisk in the square of San Giovanni in Laterano in Rome (**A**) and the obelisk in Aswan (**B**)*

42.5 m
B

33.5 m
A

The Botanical Island

O riginally called "Kitchener's Island" after the British general who first owned it, it has been developed into a botanical garden surrounded by the Nile.

A hibiscus flower

General view of the botanical island with the landing jetty

T he botanical island is known in Arabic as *Geziret al-Nabatat* or the "Island of Plants." Until 1916 it was the property of Lord Kitchener, the

One of the many palm trees on the island

A majestic avenue runs lengthways across the island, 115 meters long

commander of the British forces at the time of the war against the Mahdists, and was transformed into a botanical garden in 1928. This splendid tropical paradise covers an area of seventeen *feddans* (a feddan is the equivalent of 4200 square meters) and can be reached in just a few minutes sail from Aswan. Its hundreds of different plant species include many examples of local flora (for example, date palms, dum palms, tamarisks, acacias, papayas, and mangos) as well as species from Central and East Africa. The island is also home to many birds.

One of the herons that live on the island

St. Simeon's Monastery

This huge seventh century building, standing alone in the desert, is rarely visited by tourists, yet it was one of the largest and most important monasteries in Egypt.

The mass of St. Simeon's monastery seen from the east: the arrow indicates the entrance

St. Simeon's monastery was built in the seventh century AD on the west bank of the Nile in a high place that overlooks the river and its shores. Rebuilt and enlarged in the tenth century, the monastery was dedicated to a saint named Amba Samaan who was bishop of

The apse in the church

Aswan in the 4th–5th centuries AD.

Enclosed by solid walls 6 meters tall it seems a fortress, but this was typical of Coptic monasteries which, being built in isolated places, often had to face attack from raiders.

St. Simeon's was a self-sufficient citadel where three hundred monks lived. It was built on two levels: the lower level was entered as soon as one crossed the threshold and was equipped with a church and a dormitory for pilgrims. The church is

aligned on an east–west axis, has a triple-aisled nave, and a tripartite apse decorated with wall paintings, some parts of which are still visible, including Christ triumphant with two angels and saints. The upper level is further divided into two sections: the northeast is occupied by the kitchens, a large double-naved refectory that originally had a vaulted ceiling, and the cells of the monks which open onto a long corridor that still has its vaulted ceiling. The southern and

General view of the monastery of St. Simeon on the west bank of the Nile, surrounded by the sand of the desert

central section was reserved for the service area, the stores, the

A millstone still lies in the western part of the monastery

stalls, and the mill (the millstone is still there). Attacked and heavily damaged in 1173 by Sultan Salah al-Din, the monastery was abandoned in the thirteenth century, probably as a result of raids and problems of water supply, and was never used again. St. Simeon's can be reached in about twenty minutes by felucca and then on foot or by camel along a sandy track that passes beside the famous mausoleum built in a purely Fatimid style in which the third Aga Khan was buried in 1957. He was a descendant of Fatima, the daughter of Muhammad, the spiritual head of the Isma'ili sect of Muslims that has about five million followers.

An alternative route to the monastery is to take the track from Qubbet al-Hawa where the "Tombs of the Nobles" are to be found.

The mausoleum of the Aga Khan

The monastery of St. Simeon as it looks today

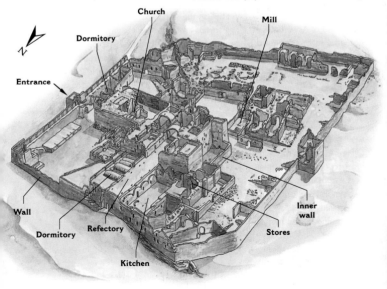

Church

Mill

Dormitory

Entrance

N

Wall

Dormitory

Refectory

Kitchen

Stores

Inner wall

The Tombs of the Nobles

Sirenput II

A series of superbly decorated tombs that are artistic treasures of the Old and Middle Kingdoms lie in the necropolis of the governors of Elephantine, situated on the hill of Qubbet al-Hawa on the west bank of the Nile.

Tombs of Mekhu and Sabni

Tomb of Sidi Ali Bin Al-Hawa

Tomb of Siremput II

Ramps

Steps

General view of the necropolis of Qubbet al-Hawa

On the west bank of the Nile opposite the north end of Aswan, a domed tomb was built for the local holy man, Sidi Ali Bin al-Hawa, on the top of a hill 180 meters high. This tranquil site, called *Contrasyene* by the Greeks and *Qubbet al-Hawa* by the Arabs ("the dome of al-Hawa"), is also the location of the necropolis of the nomarchs (governors) and other high dignitaries of Elephantine during the end of the Old Kingdom and the Middle Kingdom. The graveyard comprises about eighty tombs dug out of the sandstone of the hill on the same level. The tombs are structurally simple with an entrance court, a pillared room (not always present), a corridor, and the burial chamber; some of them are well worth a visit, as the low reliefs that decorate them are of exceptional artistic and historic interest, and in some cases their colors

The entrance to the tomb of Sirenput II

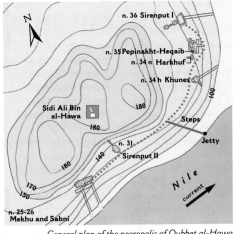

General plan of the necropolis of Qubbet al-Hawa

and his son Sabni (no. 26). **Mekhu** was a high dignitary during the reign of Pepi II (circa 2100 BC)

The main room in the tomb of Mekhu with an offering table in the foreground

have been perfectly preserved. A long flight of steps that begins near the landing stage cuts diagonally across the hill to reach the level of the tombs; these can be divided into two groups situated either south or north of the steps. The tomb of Sirenput II (no. 31) lies in the southern group and is considered one of the two most beautiful in the necropolis, along with that of Sirenput I (no. 36). **Sirenput II** was the governor of Elephantine

during the age of Amenemhat II (1920 BC); his tomb consists of a

Wall decorations in the tomb of Sirenput II: the deceased is shown sitting at the offering table with his son

Portrait of Sirenput II, a high dignitary of the Twentieth Dynasty

room with six pillars, followed by a long corridor with six niches that hold statues of the deceased, then the burial chamber with four pillars and a niche with wall paintings of the deceased with his son, his mother (on the left), and his wife (on the right). The colors of the paintings are perfectly preserved. Next door to the south are the tombs of Mekhu (no. 25)

who was given the title "hereditary prince" and lost his life during a military campaign in Nubia. The tomb is large with a main room of sixteen columns, many incomplete, arranged in three rows (no. 26), following which a corridor ends in three niches. This tomb leads into the one next door that belonged to **Sabni**, a governor of Elephantine.

Sabni, the son of Mekhu, hunts birds in the marshes

A long hieroglyphic inscription near the entrance records how the deceased had made a long expedition into the southern territories to recover the body of his father and that the pharaoh had sent embalmers from Memphis to prepare the body. The wall decorations in Sabni's tomb are fairly interesting and have retained their

twelve columns in two rows. The painting shows a hunting and fishing scene in the marshes with the deceased on a small boat accompanied by his daughters. The exteriors of both tombs have long causeways to connect them to the river for the transportation of the sarcophaguses.

The first of the northern group of tombs (no. 34h) belonged to **Khunes**, the "Chancellor of the King of Lower Egypt" during the Sixth Dynasty (2321–2140 BC). Unfortunately, it is now in a poor state having been used as a church, but it is interesting for several unusual scenes on the walls, for example, a fight between bulls. Next to this tomb is that of

Harkhuf, which is almost free of decoration inside the tomb, but of great interest for the hieroglyphs on either side of the entrance that recount three exploration expeditions made by the deceased into Upper Nubia. Harkhuf lived during the age of Merenra and his successor Pepi II. He traveled as far south

Bull-fighting scene in the tomb of Khunes

as Central Africa and on his return to Egypt, he brought a dwarf— perhaps a pygmy—with

Statue of the hereditary prince, Mekhu

polychrome colors, unlike Mekhu's tomb. One of the loveliest scenes is found in the chapel where the ceiling is supported by

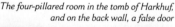

The four-pillared room in the tomb of Harkhuf, and on the back wall, a false door

The entrance to the tomb of Sirenput I with the six pillars on the façade decorated with texts and low reliefs

Low relief portraying Sirenput I

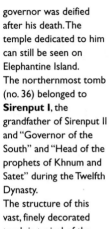

him. The texts also tell how Pepi II, when still a boy, congratulated him on the success of the expedition and was so keen

The great explorer Harkhuf

to insure the excellent health of the dwarf that he sent Harkhuf a letter of recommendation (also recounted on the outside of the tomb).

Tomb no. 35d to the north belonged to **Heqaib**, also a "Governor of Elephantine" during the Sixth Dynasty, which is distinguished by a large courtyard in front of the entrance, which is flanked by two tall, tapering pillars. A number of stelae, most of which were found in the courtyard of the tomb and which are now in Elephantine Museum, record how this

governor was deified after his death. The temple dedicated to him can still be seen on Elephantine Island.

The northernmost tomb (no. 36) belonged to **Sirenput I**, the grandfather of Sirenput II and "Governor of the South" and "Head of the prophets of Khnum and Satet" during the Twelfth Dynasty.

The structure of this vast, finely decorated tomb is typical of the Middle Kingdom, with a large court, a portico in front of the facade with six square pillars, and an entrance to the tomb in the center of the

Heqaib's tomb

portico. On either side of the door, low reliefs depict Sirenput I followed by his sandal bearer, his harem, his wife and children, and to the left, his dogs.

The interior of the tomb is a room with four pillars, a long corridor, and a second chamber with two pillars to which a niche is joined.

The Island of Philae

*C*elebrated for its beauty by travelers and artists of the nineteenth century, having been saved from the waters of the Nile, Philae continues to fascinate its visitors.

The god Hapi in his cave from which the waters of the Nile flow

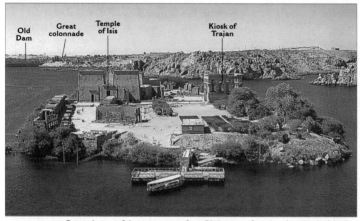

Old Dam | Great colonnade | Temple of Isis | Kiosk of Trajan

General view of the monuments from Philae transferred to the island of Agilkia

Philae, "the island of time [of Ra]" is a magical place, one of the few places in Egypt where the past still seems to be present and where Isis might still worshipped. Philae lies about eight kilometers to the south of Aswan in the stretch of the Nile between the Old and High Dams. It is opposite the island of Biga, a sacred place where one of the *Abaton* ("the inaccessible site") was believed to be, perhaps one of the sixteen tombs of the god Osiris. Moreover, it was considered to be the

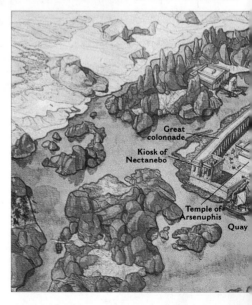

Great colonnade

Kiosk of Nectanebo

Temple of Arsenuphis

Quay

The great temple of Isis from the west

source of the Nile, the waters of which were supposed to have gushed forth from a cave below the island where the Nile god Hapi resided.

The story of Philae began in the Twenty-fifth Dynasty with the Ethiopian sovereign Taharqa (690–664 BC), who built a temple there. A few blocks of this temple have been found, while other remains belong to an early building dedicated to the cult of Isis, raised during the reign of pharaoh Amasi (570–526 BC).

The earliest complete monuments to have survived date from the Thirtieth Dynasty, the age of Nectanebo I (380–362 BC). There is a kiosk in the south-eastern section of the island that was restored by Ptolemy VIII (145–144 BC); this ruler also built a pair of obelisks in front of the first pylon in the temple of Isis that are inscribed with

The Philae monuments during the Roman times

The goddess Isis on the first pylon of her temple

The west or "great" colonnade that precedes the temple of Isis

hieroglyphs and Greek characters. One of the pair, still whole, was taken to England in 1817 by the Italian explorer Giovanni Belzoni and provided a

the Ptolemaic period, while other monuments were built during the reigns of the Roman emperors Augustus (30 BC–14 AD), Tiberius

Philae was an active center of Isis worship for almost one thousand years, and it was only when the Byzantine emperor Justinian (527–565 AD)

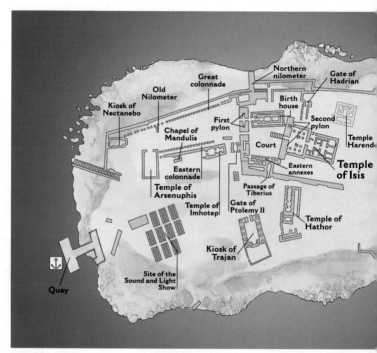

Plan of the monuments from Philae as reconstructed on Agilkia

decisive aid to Champollion in his deciphering of hieroglyphic writing.

The largest building on Philae, the **great temple of Isis**, was built during

(14–37 AD), Trajan (98–117 AD), Hadrian (117–138 AD), and Diocletian (284–305 AD), thus indicating the diffusion of the cult of Isis in the Roman empire.

decreed the closure of pagan religious buildings that the priests of Isis were obliged to leave the island (534 AD), the southernmost stronghold of the Egyptian kingdom.

The first pylon in the temple of Isis

Copts then settled there and chiseled away or destroyed many of the pagan low reliefs to

method of writing was forgotten by man for 1400 years. The temple of Isis is preceded by a majestic processional way that begins at the level of Nectanebo's kiosk. It comprised two colonnades, of which only the west "great colonnade" of thirty two columns with mixed capitals has survived complete.

Its construction was completed by Ptolemy III (246–221 BC) and it was decorated with many low reliefs during the Roman era. The imposing first pylon (38 meters wide and 18 meters tall) was built by Ptolemy V and VI (204–180 BC; 180–145 BC) and the front was decorated by Ptolemy XII

(80–51 BC) with scenes of ritual massacre by the king in the presence of Isis, Horus, and Hathor on the lower register, and of the king making offerings to Isis and Horus (to the east) and Isis and Osiris (to the west) in the upper register. The rear of the pylon (the north side) is decorated with other large low reliefs. One on the west side shows the transportation of Isis' sacred bark, which was taken every ten days to visit the tomb of her consort Osiris on the island of Biga. The gateway

The gate of Ptolemy II beside the first pylon

in the pylon was built by Nectanebo I, whose cartouches can be seen in the offering scene to Isis on the left wall in the

Temple Augustus

Gate of Diocletian

20   40   60 m

transform the temple of Isis into a church. In fact, in the year 394, an Egyptian priest carved the last hieroglyphic inscription in the history of ancient Egypt before this historic

The priests transport the sacred bark of Isis on the west side of the pylon

The second pylon of the temple of Isis: the arrow shows the large 'stele of the Dodekaschoinos'

passageway that leads to the first court. On the opposite wall, a large inscription by the sculptor Castex commemorates the arrival of the Napoleonic troops on March 3, 1799. Next to the eastern side of the pylon the Gate of Ptolemy II (285–246 BC) has an architrave decorated with scenes of offerings by the king to various gods, while on the uprights, offerings are made by the emperor Tiberius. The court built by Ptolemy II on the other side of the pylon marks the beginning of the central and oldest nucleus

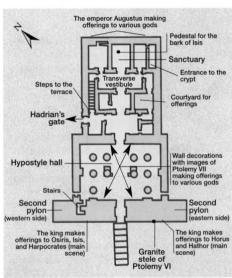

Plan of the central part of the temple of Isis

The emperor Augustus making offerings to various gods

Pedestal for the bark of Isis

Sanctuary

Entrance to the crypt

Steps to the terrace

Transverse vestibule

Courtyard for offerings

Hadrian's gate

Hypostyle hall

Wall decorations with images of Ptolemy VII making offerings to various gods

Stairs

Second pylon (western side)

Second pylon (eastern side)

The king makes offerings to Osiris, Isis, and Harpocrates (main scene)

Granite stele of Ptolemy VI

The king makes offerings to Horus and Hathor (main scene)

The birth house or mammisi

of the temple.
The west side is bounded by the **birth house** (or *mammisi*) of Ptolemy III, the decoration of which is similar in content to that of the temple at Dendera which was dedicated to Isis, the mother of Horus. Among the many low reliefs in this building is the

famous scene that shows Isis weaning Horus as a child. The north side of the court is bounded by the second, smaller pylon (14 meters high) built during the reign of Ptolemy VI, but this too was decorated by Ptolemy XII with offering scenes. Note the large granite stele of Ptolemy VI in front of the east body of the pylon; it weighs about 200 tons and records how the region known as Dodekaschoinos (from the Greek words meaning "twelve *skénes*," a unit of measure equal to 10 kilometers), that stretched 120 kilometers from *Syene* (Aswan) to *Hyera Sykaminos* (Maharraqa), was donated to the temple of Isis. Once past the second pylon, one enters the hypostyle hall with ten columns decorated with low reliefs. At the entrance, the court is open to the sky but in the inner section it is covered by a ceiling decorated with images of the goddess Nekhbet with wings spread wide and wearing the red crown of Lower Egypt and the *atef* crown.

The sanctuary of the temple with the pedestal for Isis' bark

Then comes the *naos*, comprising twelve rooms, a small court for offerings, a crypt, and a terrace from which it is possible to reach the chapel where the Osirian mysteries were celebrated. Crossing a transverse vestibule, one enters the sanctuary where the pedestal for Isis' bark stands bearing a dedication from Ptolemy III and his queen Berenice II. The eastern and western walls of this room are decorated with nine paintings that depict the pharaoh making offerings to Isis and other gods. On the north wall the king is welcomed by Harsiesi and Thoth who offer him an *ankh* sign. In the lower register, there is a procession of spirits representing the Nile, each holding a vase and preceded by the depiction of a bunch of lotus flowers and papyruses. In the sanctuary itself there were originally two pavilions that contained the sacred statues of Isis but they were removed during the nineteenth and are now in the Louvre and the British Museum.

The temple of Hathor, and in the background, Trajan's kiosk

The goddess Hathor shown on the uprights of the gate of her temple

Trajan's kiosk and the temple of Isis seen from the east

The East Bank

To the east of the temple of Isis there stands a small **temple of Hathor** built by Ptolemy VI and Ptolemy VII (145–144 BC), which was later enlarged with a vestibule during the reign of Augustus. The columns

An elaborate composite capital in Trajan's kiosk

of the building were partially destroyed during the Coptic period, spoiling the low reliefs that depict the pacification of Hathor who was sent to earth by Ra, in the guise of the lioness Sekhmet, to punish rebellious man.

The elegant **Trajan's kiosk**, which has almost become the symbol of

Philae, stands to the south of Hathor's temple. This building is nicknamed "the pharaoh's bed" by locals; it has no roof (the original covering was probably made from wood), but its fourteen columns with elaborate composite capitals are connected to each other by half-walls called *intercolumni*. The presence of two access doors, one on the east side facing the Nile, and the other on the west side, suggest that the building was related to a processional event and that it may have been a resting place for Isis' bark. The lack of epigraphic evidence, however, means its actual function cannot be confirmed. A few meters from the Nile, on the northeast corner of the island, there are the remains of the **temple of Augustus** and the monumental **Diocletian's gate** which was probably a triumphal arch.

Diocletian's gate on the northeast corner of the island

The West Bank

On the opposite bank, facing Biga island, there are several monuments of great interest, such as **Hadrian's gate**, which was built during the first half of the second century AD. Its architrave is decorated with scenes of offerings from the emperor to various gods and the reliefs in the vestibule illustrate the myth of Osiris. Also interesting is the representation of the cave of the god of the Nile, Hapi, from which, according to the beliefs of the time, the waters of the Nile flowed.

A few dozen meters south stands a **Nilometer**.

The Rescue of Philae

The first pylon of the temple of Isis half-submerged by the Nile

The temples on the island of Philae, "the pearl of Egypt," were dismantled and reassembled on the nearby island of Agilkia between 1975 and 1980.

With the construction of the first Aswan dam in 1902 and the consequent formation of a reservoir holding approximately one billion cubic meters of water, the fate of Philae was sealed.

The monuments on the island—which the French writer Pierre Loti, author of the famous *La Mort de Philae*, called the "pearl of Egypt"—were almost completely covered by the water of the Nile for most of the year. It was only during the summer months, corresponding to the flooding of the river, when the sluice gates were opened and Philae temporarily returned to sight.

When the huge "Nubia campaign" was launched by UNESCO to save the Nubian monuments destined to be submerged by construction of the new High Dam, it was decided to include the rescue of Philae in the plan.

The plan chosen called for a barrier to be built around the island so that it might dry out, then the 45,000 blocks of rock in

The pylon reassembled on Agilkia

the monuments would be dismantled and transferred to their relative original positions on Agilkia Island, which lies about 300 meters upstream. The project was carried out by the Italian firm Condotte-Mazzi Estero over the five year period 1975–80. On March 11, 1980, the new site was officially opened.

Plan showing the positions of Philae and Agilkia

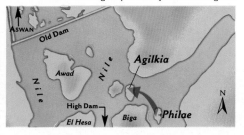

The Nubia Museum

*T*his most modern and functional of Egyptian museums offers visitors a complete panorama of the history and archeology of the region and much of Nubian culture.

*A typic
orname.*

The main entrance to the Nubia Museum

*T*he Nubia Museum is a very beautiful series of buildings that blend perfectly into the landscape. It not only displays a collection of very important objects from throughout Nubia's history, art, and culture, it is also intended to be a hub around which the cultural life of Aswan revolves.
Situated on a small green hill opposite the famous Old Cataract Hotel, the Nubia Museum was designed by the Egyptian architect

Mahmud al-Hakim and was opened in 1997.

An obelisk with four dog heads from the temple of Abu Simbel

Standing in the center of a vast garden, it has a surface area of 15.000 square meters, and is spread over several floors to adapt to the formation of the land. It is a real open-air museum with not only archeological items on display, but also indigenous plants, flowers, and shrubs, which are irrigated by a small canal replete with small waterfalls.
The main room of the museum contains more than two thousand

A water channel flows through the museum's large garden

Kingdom when, at the time of the pharaoh Khafre, the quarries of highly valued stone in the region began to be excavated for use in architecture and statues. Next come the sections that deal with the Middle Kingdom, the period dominated by an indigenous dynasty of nomarchs, and the New Kingdom, exhibiting objects saved during the Nubian campaign. An entire section of the museum is dedicated to

objects and is dominated by a colossal statue of Ramesses II that originally stood in the temple of Gerf Hussein (now under 60 meters of water). This was one of the few Nubian monuments that UNESCO's Nubian campaign was unable to save.

The exhibition route of the museum winds around this large room, beginning with a presentation on the Nubian region; it continues with a series of areas dedicated to prehistory, then archaeological finds dating from the Old

The dome of al-Mashad from the Fatimid dynasty is part of the Islamic monuments in the museum's garden

The colossal statue of Ramesses II in the form of Osiris comes from the temple of Gerf Hussein, as do the columns behind

Terracotta vases with decorations from the time of the Naqada II culture (fourth millennium BC)

Flint arrow heads

and illustrated. Of particular interest is the section dealing with Nubian prehistory, displaying Neolithic ostrich eggs, pots decorated with images of boats from the period of Naqada II (4th millennium BC), animal shaped palettes for cosmetics, and flint arrow heads. From the Old Kingdom, the most

important object exhibited is the diorite statue of Khafre (Fourth Dynasty), from the region of Toshka, which is practically identical to the better-known statue discovered in the lower temple of Khafre's

photographs and models of the rescue operations. Naturally, the other periods of Nubia's long history are richly documented

Animal shaped palette for cosmeticsfrom the time of the Naqada II (fourth millennium BC)

The main exhibition hall in Aswan Museum

Prehistory

Model of th Nile vall

Stairs to the main exhibition hall

Folk heritage

Folk herita

Neolithic ax head

Wooden sarcophagus of Heqata (Middle Kingdom)

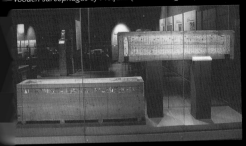

Detail of the inscriptions on the sarcophagus of Heqata

Low relief of Ramesses I making offerings to Osiri

Headless diorite statue of Khafre (Fourth Dynasty) from the site of Toshka

pyramid in Giza nearly 1,500 kilometers away, and now on display in the Egyptian Museum in Cairo. There are numerous items from the New Kingdom, many of which were found at Abu Simbel, for example a sun worshipping, dog-headed baboon that bears a sun disk on its head. Also from the New Kingdom is the elegant *ushabti* (magical statuettes that were

placed in the tomb) belonging to Heqa-nefer, the governor of Nubia. More recent are the lovely statuettes of the God's Wives of Amun who held royal power in the Theban region during the Twenty-fifth and Twentysixth Dynasties.

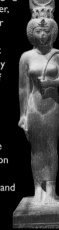

Statuette of Ankhnesneferibre, God's Wife of Amun (Twenty-sixth Dynasty)

Sarcophagus of Heqata

Chapel of Usertatet (from Qasr Ibrim)

Finds from Qustol and Ballana tombs

Model of Philae

The colossal statue of Ramesses II (Gerf Hussein)

Christian Nubia

Islamic Nubia

UNESCO Campaign

Ushabti *belonging to Heqa-nefer, the governor of Nubia, from the region of Toshka*

The most artistic of these statuettes is that of Ankhnesneferibre. The small statue of Harwa is another fine example of the sculpture of this period, which was characterized by a return to forms that sometimes showed archaistic tendencies.

A sun-worshiping baboon from Abu Simbel

The high priest Horemakhet

Head of King Shabaka (Twenty-fifth Dynasty, 712–698 BC)

Harwa was the "Chief steward of the God's Wife Amenirdis I" whose large tomb can be seen in the Theban necropolis (TT 37). This was also the period during which one of the museum's finest statues was sculpted. It is of the High Priest of Amun at Thebes, Horemakhet, Shabaka's other child. Shabaka was a Nubian king who reigned from 715–698 BC and succeeded in extending his power throughout Egypt. The museum has a head of Shabaka sculpted in pink granite that stands close to the bust of the

Funerary mask of a mummy covered in gold foil from Elephantine

pharaoh Taharqa. This section of the museum also contains many sarcophaguses and gilded funerary masks from the Late Period which were made using the cartonnage technique.

A large wooden, gold lined sarcophagus of a ram comes from the necropolis of the sacred rams on Elephantine Island.

The necropolis, which lies between the temples of Satet and Khnum, was where these animals, sacred to Khnum, were buried during the Ptolemaic period.

The route around the museum continues with finds from the main necropolises of the princes of Qustol and Ballana that reigned in the region during the fourth and sixth centuries: the finds include three finely decorated silver crowns and the caparisons of horses in which the animals were buried. A following section is dedicated to the Christian period during which important religious centers were built in Nubia—the three tenth century

Schist statue of Harwa "Chief steward of the God's Wife Amenirdis I" (Twenty-fifth Dynasty) from Karnak

Sarcophagus of a ram covered in gold foil, from the necropolis of sacred rams on Elephantine Island

frescoes from the church of Abdallah Nerque are of special interest—and then a section on the age of Islamic Nubia which began in the second half of the seventh century. A surprise awaits the visitor in the final section, which focuses on the Nubian culture, which has links with those of central Africa and Upper Nubia (Sudan). The characteristics of Nubian

the museum using the materials typical of the region—unfired bricks and sand—and decorated with motifs and objects that are traditional to the Nubian culture, for example, birds, animals, flags, and plates. Some life-sized figures of a man teaching the Koran to a pupil help bring this lovely diorama to life. Craft objects in the displays include a fine quality sword in a leather sheath and plates made

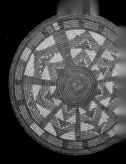

Typical Nubian plate made from colored palm leaves woven to create geometric patterns

Silver crown from Ballana necropolis (third–sixth century BC), example of the Meroitic art with Byzantine influences

Nubian sword

culture are very different from those to be seen in the Nile Valley or the oases of the Libyan Desert. A complete Nubian house has been built in

from painted palm leaves woven to form

geometric patterns. Art, architecture, and crafts are elements that, along with music and dance, most exemplify the popular culture of Aswan and, in general, all of Lower Nubia.

Reconstruction of a typical Nubian house inside the museum

ESSENTIAL BIBLIOGRAPHY

Baines, J., J. Malek. *Atlas of Ancient Egypt*. Oxford -Nex York, 1980.

Curto, S. *Nubia*. Novara, 1965.

de Rochemonteix M. and Chassinat E., *Le temple d'Edfou*. 14 vols, Paris, 1892; Cairo, 1918-.

de Morgan J. et al., *Kom Ombos*. 2 vols, Vienna, 1909.

Kamil J., *Aswan and Abu Simbel*. Cairo, 1993.

Porter, B., R.L.B. Moss. *Topographical Bibliography of Ancient Egyptian Hierogliphic Texts, Reliefs and Paintings*. 7 vols., Oxford, 1927.

Sauneron, S. *Esna I-*. Cairo, 1959-67.

Siliotti, A. *Egypt—Temples, Men, and Gods*. Cairo, 2001.

Taylor, J.H. *Egypt and Nubia*. London, 1991.

Junker H., WInter E., *Philä*. Vienna, 1958-.

Vassilika, E., *Ptolemaic Philae*. Leuven, 1989.

Wilkinson R.H., *The Complete Temples of Ancient Egypt*. London, 2000.

PHOTOGRAPH CREDITS

All the photographs in this book are by Alberto Siliotti/Archivio Image Service-Geodia except

Courtesy Condotte Mazzi (Italy): page 41.

DRAWINGS

Stefania Cossu: pages 5, 8, 20, 21, 29, 36-37.

Melissa Frigotto: 3rd page of cover, pages 10-11, 12-13, 17.

Jean Claude Golvin/Errance Éd.: pages 7 above, 34-35.

Stefano Trainito: pages 44-45.